Railway Company Canada Southern

The Canada Southern Railway

Extending from Detroit and Toledo to Buffalo and Niagara Falls

Railway Company Canada Southern

The Canada Southern Railway
Extending from Detroit and Toledo to Buffalo and Niagara Falls

ISBN/EAN: 9783337147594

Printed in Europe, USA, Canada, Australia, Japan

Cover: Foto ©Andreas Hilbeck / pixelio.de

More available books at **www.hansebooks.com**

The Canada Southern Railway,

EXTENDING FROM

DETROIT AND TOLEDO

TO

BUFFALO AND NIAGARA FALLS,

FORMS THE

Quickest and most Attractive Route

BETWEEN

THE WEST AND THE EAST.

THIS COMPANY

Has placed on sale at Detroit, Toledo, Columbus, Dayton, Cincinnati, Louisville, Nashville, Chattanooga, Atlanta, Indianapolis, St. Louis, Kansas City, Chicago, Grand Rapids, Saginaw, Bay City, St. Thomas, Buffalo, and other principal cities of the West and South, a full line of Summer Excursion Tickets, via the most attractive Routes, to all Resorts in the Eastern States.

The following Agents of the Canada Southern Railway Co. will cheerfully reply to any inquiries respecting Rates and Routes:

W. H. HURLBURT,
Gen'l West. Pass. Ag't,
CHICAGO, ILL.

M. C. ROACH,
Western Pass. Ag't,
DETROIT, MICH.

WM. GATES,
Ticket Ag't, Boody House,
TOLEDO, OHIO.

C. A. WARREN,
Pass. & Ticket Ag't,
154 Jeff. Ave., DETROIT, MICH.

E. H. HUBBARD,
Eastern Pass. Ag't,
BUFFALO, N. Y.

H. M. HUNTER,
Pass. & Ticket Agent,
ST. THOMAS, ONT.

W. P. TAYLOR,
General Manager,
BUFFALO, N. Y.

FRANK E. SNOW,
Gen'l Pass. & Ticket Ag't,
BUFFALO, N. Y.

DEVIL'S OVEN, THOUSAND ISLANDS.

The Canada Southern Railway.

A few Notes of Interest Along the Line.

OMMENCING our journey at Toledo, it is less than an hour's ride up the shore of Lake Erie, and past the beautiful town of Monroe, to the mouth of Detroit River, where crossing the American channel upon a fine bridge we reach the lovely

GROSSE ISLE.

This charming island is a favorite summer resort, and contains many costly and elegant residences built by prominent business men of Detroit, Toledo and Cincinnati. The place is so delightful that some of these lovers of pure air have become permanent residents, remaining in their beautiful cottages all the year round. The train from Detroit arrives here at the same time as the one from Toledo, and the two, including through cars from St. Louis and Chicago, are transferred entire upon immense Iron Ferry Steamers, to Amherstburg, and continue to Buffalo and Niagara Falls as one train.

AMHERSTBURG,

Formerly known as Malden, lies at the mouth of Detroit River, and is of some historic interest—the ruins of Fort Malden, and a well preserved and picturesque old Block House, on Bois Blanc Island, still remaining to remind us of the days of Tecumseh, and the eloquent appeals of the Indian Statesman, Logan, who spent his last days here.

The view at this point is very fine, and whoever goes east without seeing the beautiful islands and noble expanse of the Detroit, has to regret the loss of one of the finest river views in America.

BRIDGE AND DRIVE, GROSSE ILE.

From Amherstburg to St. Thomas, a distance of 111 miles, the road has but one curve, and was the scene of the famous run of Sept. 13th, 1877, of which the following account appeared in the DETROIT FREE PRESS:

111 MILES IN 109 MINUTES.

A TRAIN THAT LEFT A WHIRLWIND IN ITS WAKE.

The clergy and leading members of the various societies of Detroit were desirous of tendering to the returning Bishop a public

COTTAGE AT GROSSE ISLE.

reception. The time of the arrival of the regular trains from the East not being sufficiently early to permit of that object, Gen'l Passenger Agent FRANK E. SNOW, of the Canada Southern, tendered a special train to convey them to St. Thomas, there to meet Bishop BORGESS, and escort him to Detroit on a train which should arrive in advance of the regular train.

The committee accepted this offer, and at noon of September 13th, 1877, they left Detroit, proceeded to St. Thomas, and awaited the arrival of the Bishop, for the purpose of transferring him to the special train in waiting to convey him to Detroit.

BLOCK HOUSE, DETROIT RIVER.

There was to be only one stop in the hundred and eleven miles that separate St. Thomas from Amherstburg. The engineer, Macomber, was surrounded by an admiring throng, which commented on the handsome appearance of his iron steed. He attended to the oiling of the engine and the "doping" of the journals and boxes, and his whole demeanor affirmed his determination to make "the run through by the card." The steam gauge, just before starting, showed a pressure of eighty-five pounds. The air-brake cylinders clucked in an impatient manner

BRIDGE AT ST. THOMAS.

and the light smoke ascended perpendicularly in the still air of the delightful September afternoon.

The fireman was pointed out by an acquaintance. "He's a stout young fellow," said he, "as you see, but there'll be nothing but a grease spot left of him by the time the train reaches Amherstburg; that is, if Macomber tries to beat Vanderbilt's time, for this train is one car heavier than Vanderbilt's."

"Oh, don't you talk," said another; "the run there and back on that engine won't warm him up. What's two hours of firing?"

This conversation, and these preparations, excited a number of the more timorous passengers. A half dozen of them made straight for the ticket-office and purchased accident insurance tickets.

General Manager Muir heard of it. "Why," said he, "that's preposterous. There is but one curve in our track between here and the Detroit River, and that's at Charing Cross, where we stop

DEPOT, ST. THOMAS.

for water. The road-bed is in perfect condition, there are no bridges once we leave the town, and the rails are of the heaviest steel on any railroad in America. Our rolling stock is first-class. I'm going to Detroit in that train."

The Pacific Express came up; Conductor Crawford sang out "all aboard!" and the special pulled out from St. Thomas at 5.27 P. M. A grand hurrah from the platform signaled the departure.

Once the bridge was cleared Macomber "let her out." In the palace car the party sat down, and dinner was served upon a small

table. No one noticed any particular motion in the car. There
was no disarrangement of the dishes, crowded and small as was
the table. The hum of the train was somewhat sharper than usual,
and the rushing air against the windows sounded like the sweep-
ing of a rain-storm. Otherwise there was no indication of unusual
speed to a person in the car.

Presently watches were taken out and observations made.

"A mile in sixty seconds!" ejaculated one.

Shortly after — "A mile in fifty-eight seconds!"

Again — "A mile in fifty-seven seconds!" and Fred. Moran,
with a cheer, announced that his stop-watch marked but fifty-three
seconds to the mile.

At the rear end of the last coach sat General Manager Muir,
his eyes fixed on the ever-appearing, ever-vanishing track, with a
demeanor philosophic, as if such speed was an every-day affair on
the Canada Southern.

Before one could point out an object it had vanished. Before
a question could be asked and answered a mile had sped.

The wires on the telegraph poles swung up and down from the
movement of the train The bushes on the side of the ditches
shook as if swept by a hurricane. A thin line of smoke stretched
interminably in the distance. The impetus of the train increased;
the vehemence with which it rushed forward created a vacuum
that apparently took nature some seconds to overcome, and the
spirits of the passengers were exhilerated by the unprecedented
speed at which they moved through space.

A side-tracked passenger train saluted with cheers and locomotive whistles. Neither was heard; before the sound could reach
the ears of the passengers in the special it was beyond hearing.
One could see the rushing steam and the waving handkerchiefs.
Six miles between Highgate and Ridgetown were made in five
minutes; the fifty-seven miles between St. Thomas and Charing
Cross were made in fifty-six and a half minutes. A halt at Charing Cross of four minutes for water, and then on again with the
same overpowering velocity. But go as fast as it might, the train
could not overtake the sun; it sank and nightfall came on. Then
could be seen the work of the fireman. Each time he opened the
furnace a volume of sparks shot out, and the trailing fire came
down upon the track like the pyrotechnics of an aerial mine.

Finally, a sharp twist that sent the standing passengers over
to the right, and directly another that sent then in another direc-
tion, and the yard of Amherstburg station was reached.

Hurrah! One hundred and eleven miles in one hundred and
nine minutes! The fastest time in America—beating by three
minutes the remarkable run of Vanderbilt's special train."

The run from Amherstburg to Fort Erie, two hundred and twen-
ty-nine miles was made on May 5, '81 with Mr. Cornelius Vanderbilt

GRAND RIVER, DEANS.

and party of New York Capitalists in two hundred and thirty five
minutes by the Celebrated Fontaine Locomotive, a cut of which
appears on the opening page of this guide.

ST. THOMAS.

One of the most prosperous and beautiful cities of Canada,
containing many fine residences and lovely drives. The general
offices and machine shops of the company are located here. The
Canada Southern Dining Hall, where all trains stop for meals,
has no superior in the country.

OLD WINDMILL, FORT ERIE.

HAMILTON,

A city of considerable importance, is reached via a branch line of twenty-six miles from Hagersville.

Burlington Beach is a favorite lakeside resort.

GRAND RIVER.

At Deans an iron bridge spans this beautiful river. Here the
Chiefs of the several tribes of Chippewas, Oneidas, Senecas and
Muncy Indians met in council each year, it being the home of the
Chiefs of the several Nations.

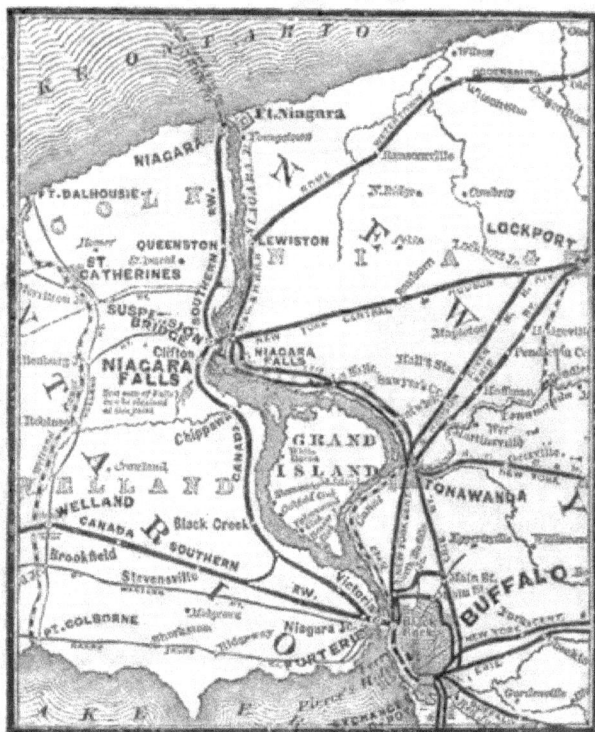

WELLAND.

The great Welland Ship Canal which connects Lake Erie with
Ontario, is crossed at this point, and a short ride brings the traveler
to

BUFFALO,

Where Canada Southern trains connect with all trains of the N.
Y. Central and N. Y., L. E. & W. R'ys. If the tourist wishes to

GLIMPSE OF AMERICAN FALLS, FROM C. S. TRAIN.

go East, by Niagara Falls, he continues his journey over the
Niagara Falls Division, which runs down the bank of Niagara
River, past the battle grounds of Chippewa and Lundy's Lane, to

HORSESHOE FALLS AND RAPIDS, FROM C. S. TRAIN.

NIAGARA FALLS.

A large platform has been erected on the brink of the chasm,
just at the foot of the Rapids, and all trains stop ten minutes,

giving passengers time to experience **that supreme** sense **of awe** which characterizes the view from this point.

It is well known that many people visit Niagara, and, **after** being hustled about the hotels, and driven **over the** beaten **paths** of the hackmen, come away with a lingering sense of disappointment. The Falls did not impress them as **they** had expected; and, though recognizing the truth of all the glorious descriptions they have read and heard, they feel that there is something lacking, something in Niagara that was **not** exhibited to them — and they are right. **They have not seen the** crowning majesty **of** that great cataract, **or felt the** overwhelming, awe inspiring sensation excited **by** that first **view from** the bluff.

Horseshoe Falls, from the Clifton, are picturesque; **American** Falls, from **Cave of the** Winds, are awful; the Great **Chasm is** wonderful, **and the Rapids terrible;** but the vast expanse **of Rapids** and **Islands and Falls and Gorge, as seen in** one **comprehensive** view **from the Canada Southern platform, is sublime and su**preme. **It is the incarnation of all that is grand,** wonderful **and** awe inspiring in **Niagara; and happy is he who gets his** first impressions of the great cataract from that **point, which has long** been chosen **by Poets and** Painters as the **best for artistic study.** It might indeed **be well** named *Inspiration Point*.

The Canada **Southern is** positively **the only line from the West that lands** passengers directly **at the Falls.**

A Transfer Company has been organized for the protection of the traveling public. An agent will board each **train**, before reaching the Falls, and recheck baggage, and provide transfer tickets to any hotel **on the Canada or** American side, at rate **of** fifty cents for one passenger and usual amount of baggage. Continuing trip down the **Mountain** from Niagara **Falls, a fine view** of the battle field of Queenston Heights is **had from** the train. Brock's monument, a stately column erected in honor of **a British** General of that **name,** stands upon **the heights** near the railway.

OLD NIAGARA,

The terminus of the Canada Southern **R'y, is** next reached; once the Capital of Upper Canada but now a favorite resort for citizens

of Toronto and Buffalo. The pleasures of fishing, boating, bath-
ing, of good roads and pleasant drives attract many visitors during
the summer months. The Queen's Royal Hotel, delightfully
situated near the beach, affords the very best accommodations for
tourists. Here also may be seen the dismantled British Forts,
Niagara and Moss. Opposite stands Fort Niagara, with the Stars
and Stripes overhead.

From Old Niagara three elegant steamers run daily to Toronto,
affording a pleasant trip, of two hours, across beautiful Lake
Ontario.

TORONTO

Justly claims the proud title of "The Queen City of Canada,"
and contains many beautiful and costly public buildings. The
University, Trinity College, Normal School, Lorretto Convent,
English and Catholic Cathedrals, the Lt. Governor's residence,
Parliament buildings, Art Gallery, etc. The city has also many
lovely drives, among them the Queen's Park.

LAKES OF MUSKOKA.

From Toronto, these lovely lakes are reached via the Northern
R'y; they have long been known as a favorite summer resort.

DOWN THE ST. LAWRENCE.

During the summer months the Richelieu & Ontario Navigation Company dispatch every afternoon, at two o'clock, one of
their elegant side wheel steamers from Toronto (Canada Southern
Wharf) for the St. Lawrence trip. Those who desire to do so
can take train from Toronto with sleepers attached to Kingston
where connection is made next morning with steamer. The far-
famed Thousand Islands appear in sight soon after leaving Kingston. No where in the world are more beautiful scenes presented
than during the trip through these lovely islands. As the steamer
glides through the intricate channels, each moment reveals new
beauties, making the whole trip of the most enchanting interest.

Commencing June 20th, '81, the St. Lawrence Steamboat
Company will run a line of Steamers from Cape Vincent, N. Y.

QUEEN'S ROYAL HOTEL, NIAGARA.

to Montreal, leaving Cape Vincent 6.30 a. m., arriving at Montreal 5.30 p. m. same day, touching at Alexandria Bay and other intermediate points, and connecting at Montreal with all Railroad and Steamboat lines.

ALEXANDRIA BAY

Is the chief summer resort of the St. Lawrence. The numerous islands in the immediate neighborhood contain many fine resi-

VIEW IN THOUSAND ISLANDS.

dences, among others, "Bonniecastle," the summer home of Dr. J. G. Holland. Several fine hotels afford ample accommodations for tourists.

LONG SAULT RAPIDS,

About ten miles in length, are next reached The current rushes through them at the rate of twenty miles an hour, and the descent is exciting in the extreme.

LACHINE RAPIDS,

The shortest but swiftest encountered in the St. Lawrence. Here the Indian Pilot, whose fame is known to all who make the leap

FIDDLER'S ELBOW, THOUSAND ISLANDS.

down the perilous descent, has for many years safely guided boats down the Rapids, to the admiration and delight of all travelers. After passing the Rapids, and steaming under the great Victoria Bridge, costing $6,300,000,

MONTREAL,

The commercial metropolis of Canada, is reached.   A sojourn of several days here will repay the traveler.   Montreal contains many magnificent buildings — the new Post Office, Banks, Mechanics' Institute, new Court House, McGill College, Bonsecours

FAIRY LAND, THOUSAND ISLANDS.

Market, and the Cathedral of Notre Dame, the largest church edifice in North America.   On St. Catherine street is situated the English Cathedral, the most perfect specimen of Gothic architecture in the country. The Windsor and St. Lawrence Hall Hotels are well known to the traveling public. Montreal has many delightful drives; one to the top of Mount Royal gives a

LONG SAULT RAPIDS.

splendid view of the city and river. Longue Point should not be omitted, and a drive to Lachine, along the river bank, in full view of the rapids, returning via boat running the rapids, is a trip high- ly appreciated by visitors.

QUEBEC.

Magnificent steamers leave Montreal every evening, except Sunday, reaching Quebec early the following morning. The rail route is G. T. R'y, via Richmond, or Q., M., O. & O. R'y — each line running two daily trains.

RUSH OF WATERS, LONG SAULT RAPIDS.

No city on the continent so impresses the tourist, by startling peculiarities of site and the novelty of its general aspect, as this "Ancient Capital." Its antique buildings, lovely drives and historical scenes, make it one of the most attractive resorts on the

American continent. Among the many scenes that will interest the tourist, may be mentioned the ancient gates dividing the city; the cottage where Montcalm had his headquarters at the time of the celebrated battle with Wolfe; Durham Terrace, affording a view considered by many as second to none in America; Duf-

LACHINE RAPIDS.

ferin Terrace, named after Lord Dufferin, late Gov. General of Canada, and which forms one of the grandest promenades in the world; the Governor's Garden, containing the monument erected in memory of those two brave Commanders, Wolfe and Mont-calm, who, though in life brought into deadly enmity, are united in the memories of the future; the Grand Battery; the Esplanade; the English Cathedral; the Ursuline Convent, founded early in the seventeenth century, with its fine paintings ; the University of Quebec ; Laval University ; French Cathedral, etc., are all open to visitors, and will be found of great interest.

Wolfe's Monument, on the plains of Abraham, where he fell ; a trip to the Isle of Orleans ; the lovely drive of several miles. through the French villages to the Falls of Montmorenci, with its beautiful scenery, will well repay the traveler. The best hotels are the St. Louis and the Russell. The trip from Quebec down the St. Lawrence, and up the far-famed

EVENING.

SAGUENAY RIVER,

To Cacouna, Tadousac, Murray Bay, Cape Eternity and Ha Ha Bay, is considered one of the finest in America. Steamers for the Saguenay trip leave Quebec every morning, except Sunday, during the summer months.

LAKE CHAMPLAIN.

Leaving Montreal in the morning, a ride of two hours by rail brings the traveler to Plattsburg, where steamers are in waiting to make the trip down the lake to Ticonderoga, passing enroute many scenes of great historic interest. Those who desire can,

however, pursue their journey by the Delaware and Hudson
Canal Co. R'y, to Baldwin, at the head of

LAKE GEORGE.

The American Tourist is familiar with the repeated and glow-
ing descriptions of this beautiful lake, with its romantic islands

LAKE GEORGE.

and transparent waters ; but neither the unrivaled scenery nor the
ceaseless play of light and shade upon its rock-bound islets and

coasts, can for a moment equal the absorbing interest excited by the historic legends of this memorable region.

SARATOGA.

From Fort William Henry Hotel, Lake George, the trip over the mountains on the Tally Ho Stage, to Glen's Falls, is picturesque and exciting, and will be thoroughly enjoyed by all. The driver will point out many spots of historical interest. From Glen's Falls D. & H. C. Co.'s trains run direct to Saratoga.

MOONRISE.

DOWN THE HUDSON.

During the summer months a special train leaves Saratoga every morning, connecting with Day Line Steamers at Albany, making the famous and delightful trip "Down the Hudson, to New York, by Day Light."

CONEY ISLAND,

The most popular sea-side resort in the United States, is but ten miles from New York, and easily reached by any one of fifteen or twenty routes in forty-five minutes. It is not uncommon to see 150,000 people on the island at one time ; and some sixty hotels and five thousand bath houses are required for their accommodation.

The remarkable gradation of fashion and differences of social usage exhibited in the four miles of Coney island hotels and beach are never failing sources of amusement and interest to every observer of human nature. From the refined elegance and luxurious fashion of the Oriental and Manhattan, it is but two or three hours walk through the popular and intermediate phases of Brighton and West Brighton, to the free-and-easy frolic of Norton's at the lower end of the island.

CAPE MAY AND LONG BRANCH.

Through tickets, via St. Lawrence, Lake George and White Mountains, to these charming summer coast resorts. See list of forms.

OLD MAN OF THE MOUNTAIN.

THROUGH THE WHITE MOUNTAINS.

The Canada Southern Tickets, via the St. Lawrence, Montreal and Quebec, consist of numerous forms, and read via all lines to Boston, Portland and New York, with side trips to all places of interest in the Mountains, including trips up Mt. Washington to Tip Top House, Profile House, Bethlehem, Franconia, Twin Mountain House, Crawford House, Glen House and through the Notch; from Newport, a trip up Lake Memphremagog; from Weirs, a delightful trip on Lake Winnepiseogee to Centre Harbor, and Wolfboro; and other short trips to resorts of pleasure throughout the White Mountain district, extending on to Old Orchard Beach, Mt. Desert, Nantucket, Rye Beach, Newport, Narragansett Pier, Martha's Vinyard, etc.

SPECIAL NOTICE

Tickets between Toronto and Montreal, reading via Richelieu and Ontario Navigation Co.'s Steamers are not good via Rail.

Forms reading via Rail from Toronto are valid on Steamers from Kingston to Montreal. Parties desiring can take Pullman Sleeper at Toronto, which is run directly to Kingston wharf (allowing full night's rest) where boat may be taken at 6.00 A. M.

Tickets on Steamers include meals (berths extra) between Toronto and Montreal. Between Montreal, Quebec and Saguenay River points, meals and berths extra.

Tickets on Lake Champlain and Lake George Steamers, meals extra.

Tickets on Hudson River and Sound Steamers, meals and berths extra.

Tickets from Plattsburg to Fort Ticonderoga are valid either via Rail or Boat.

Tickets reading over Mt. Washington R'y, are valid only from 1st of June to 1st of October.

The Hudson River, Lake Champlain and Lake George Steamers commence their trips about the 1st of June, and after October 1st trips are irregular.

SPECIAL TICKETS ARRANGED.

The Canada Southern Railway Company, in addition to the large variety of Summer Excursion Tickets, will arrange Special Tickets to any resort in the East not noted in this book. Agents of this Company will cheerfully reply to all applications, and give rates and all information required, and will also accompany parties of ten or more to look after their comfort and arrange all details for a pleasure trip.

RESERVED STATE-ROOMS.

The Canada Southern Company has arranged with the Richelieu and Ontario Navigation Co. to reserve state-rooms on St. Lawrence Steamers, from Toronto, on application from our Agents. Parties desiring such accommodation should apply by letter to Canada Southern Agent, or call on Ticket Agent of connecting lines as per list attached. This arrangement will be found of great use, as state-rooms may be secured several days in advance.

Remember no other line offers this inducement.

MOUNT WASHINGTON RAILWAY.

WATKINS GLEN.

Canada Southern Railway.

ROUTES AND RATES.

ROUTE 1—To Boston.

Via Niagara Falls, Niagara, Toronto, River St. Lawrence.

Form.

P. 731 Canada Southern R'y.................to Niagara
Steamer..................................to Toronto
Richelieu & Ont. Nav. Co. Steamer to Montreal

Or via Niagara Falls, Niagara, Toronto, Kingston and River St. Lawrence.

1012 Ex. Canada Southern R'y.................to Niagara
Steamer..................................to Toronto
Grand Trunk R'y............. ......to Kingston
Gr. Trunk R'y or Rich. & Ont. N. Co. to Montreal

Or via Niagara Falls, Lewiston, Cape Vincent, Alexandria Bay and Rapids of St. Lawrence.

1059 Ex. Canada Southern R'y ....to Niagara Falls
N. Y. Central & Hudson River R. R. to Lewiston
Rome, Watertown & Ogd. R. R. to Cape Vincent
St. Lawrence Steamboat Co. Steamer to Montreal

Or via Buffalo or Niagara Falls, Syracuse, Cape Vincent, Alexandria Bay and Rapids of St. Lawrence.

1013 Ex. Canada Southern R'y to Buffalo or Niagara Falls
N. Y. Central & Hudson River R. R. to Syracuse
Rome, Watertown & Ogd. R. R. to Cape Vincent
Steamer.......................to Alexandria Bay
Richelieu & Ont. Nav. Co. Steamer..to Montreal

1001 Ex. South-Eastern R'y...................to Newport   *Via Toronto.*
Passumpsic R. R. ....to Wells River   20.00 24.00 25.70
Boston, Concord & Montreal R. R....to Concord *Via Cape Vincent,*
Concord R. R. ....to Nashua *or Rail to Kingston.*
Boston & Lowell R. R.................to Boston 21.00 22.70

THROUGH RATE

ROUTE 2—To Boston.

| | From Niag-
ara Falls. | From
Detroit. | From
Toledo. |

Via Montreal, Newport, Fabyans and North Conway.

Form.		From Niag- ara Falls.	From Detroit.	From Toledo.
1002 Ex	Via P. 731,1012 Ex.,1059 Ex. or 1013 Ex. to Montreal			
	South-Eastern R'y...................to Newport			
	Passumpsic R. R.................to St. Johnsbury			
	St. Johnsbury & L. Champlain R. R. to Lunenburg	*Via Toronto.*		
	Portland & Ogdensburg R. R.....to Scott's Mills	20.00	24.00	25.70
	Boston, Concord & Montreal R. R....to Fabyans	*Via Cape Vincent,*		
	Portland & Ogdensburg R. R. to North Conway	*or Rail to Kingston.*		
	Eastern R. R.......... ....to Boston	......	21.00	22.70

CAPE ETERNITY, SAGUENAY RIVER.

ROUTE 3—To Boston.

Via Montreal, **Newport**, Fabyans, Portland and Old Orchard Beach.

		Via Toronto.		
1003 Ex.	Via P. 731,1012 Ex.,1059 Ex. or 1013 Ex. to Montreal			
	South-Eastern R'y...................to Newport			
	Passumpsic R. R.................to St. Johnsbury			
	St. Johnsbury & L. Champlain R. R. to Lunenburg	*Via Toronto.*		
	Portland & Ogdensburg R. R.....to Scott's Mills	20.00	24.00	25.70
	Boston, Concord & Montreal R. R....to Fabyans	*Via Cape Vincent,*		
	Portland & Ogdensburg R. R.........to Portland	*or Rail to Kingston.*		
	Boston & Maine or Eastern R. R..... .to Boston	......	21.00	22.70

ROUTE 4—To Boston.

THROUGH RATE

From Niag-   From   From
ara Falls.   Detroit.   Toledo.

Via Montreal, Quebec, Sherbrooke, St. Johnsbury, Fabyans, North Conway.

Form.   **Via P. 731**, 1012 Ex., 1059 Ex. or 1013 Ex. to Montreal
1007 Ex. Gr. Trunk R'y or Rich.& Ont. Nav. Co. to Quebec
Grand Trunk R'y......................to Sherbrooke
Passumpsic R. R.................to St. Johnsbury
St. Johnsbury & Lake Champ. **R. R.** to Lunenburg   *Via Toronto.*
Portland & Ogdensburg R. R.....to Scott's Mills   24.00   28.00   29.70
Boston, Concord & Montreal **R. R....to** Fabyans *Via Cape Vincent,*
Portland & Ogdensburg R. R.. **to North** Conway   *or Rail to Kingston.*
Eastern R. R.............................to Boston 25.00   26.70

ROUTE 5—To Boston.

Via Montreal, Quebec, Sherbrooke, Gorham, Portland.

Via P. 731, 1012 Ex., **1059 Ex.** or 1013 Ex. to Montreal   *Via Toronto.*
1008 Ex. **Gr. Trunk R'y** or Rich. & Ont. Nav. Co. to Quebec   23.00   27.00   28.70
Grand Trunk R'y.....................to Portland   *Via Cape Vincent,*
                                                      or Rail to Kingston.
Boston & Maine or Eastern R'y........to Boston **24.00**   25.70

ROUTE 6—To Boston.

Via **Montreal**, Plattsburg, Lake Champlain, **Fort Ticonderoga, Lake** George, Glens Falls, Saratoga, Albany.

Via P. 731, 1012 Ex., 1059 Ex. or 1013 Ex. to Montreal
1005 Ex. Grand Trunk R'y..............to Rouse's Point
Delaware & Hud. Canal Co.'s R. R..to Plattsburg
Champ. Trans. Co.'s Steamer..to Ft. Ticonderoga
Delaware & Hudson Canal Co.'s R. R..to Baldwin
Lake George Steamer................to Caldwell   *Via Toronto.*
Glens Falls Stages.................to Glens Falls   28.65   31.65   33.35
Delaware & Hudson Canal Co.'s R. R..to Albany   *Via Cape Vincent,*
                                                or Rail to Kingston.
Boston & Albany R. R.................**to** Boston 29.65   31.35

ROUTE 7—To Boston.

Via Montreal, Plattsburg, Lake Champlain, **Fort** Ticonderoga, Lake George, **Glens Falls, Saratoga,** Troy, Hoosac Tunnel.

Via P. 731, 1012 Ex., 1059 Ex. or 1013 Ex. to Montreal
1006 Ex. Grand Trunk R'y................to Rouse's Point
Delaware & Hud. Canal Co.'s R. R..to Plattsburg
Champ. Trans. Co.'s Steamer..to Ft. Ticonderoga
Delaware & Hudson Canal Co.'s R.R..to Baldwin
Lake George Steamer...............to Caldwell   *Via Toronto.*
Glens Falls Stages.................to Glens Falls 28.50   31.50   33.20
Delaware & Hudson **Canal** Co.'s R. R....to Troy *Via Cape Vincent,*
Troy & Boston R. R.............to North Adams   *or Rail to Kingston.*
Fitchburg R. R.........................to Boston 29.50   **31**.20

THROUGH RATE
From Niag- From From
ara Falls. Detroit. Toledo.

ROUTE 8—To Boston.

Via Buffalo or Niagara Falls, Schenectady, Rutland and Bellows Falls.

Form.
* H. 558 Canada Southern R'y to Buffalo or Niagara Falls
N. Y. Cent. & Hud. Riv. R. R....to Schenectady
Delaware & Hudson Canal Co.'s R. R. to Rutland
Central Vermont R. R..........To Bellows Falls
Cheshire R. R...................... .to Fitchburg
Fitchburg R. R.....................to Boston 17.00   18.25

ROUTE 9—To Boston.

Via Buffalo or Niagara Falls, Rochester, Albany, Springfield & Worcester.

* H. 449 Canada Southern R'y to Buffalo or Niagara Falls
New York Central & Hudson Riv. R. R. to Albany
Boston & Albany R. R.................to Boston 17.00   18.25

ROUTE 10—To Boston.

Via Buffalo or Niagara Falls, Rochester, Troy and Hoosac Tunnel.

* H. 659 Canada Southern R'y to Buffalo or Niagara Falls
New York Central & Hudson River R. R. to Troy
Troy & Boston R. R.............to North Adams
Fitchburg R. R.......................to Boston 17.00   18.25

ROUTE 11—To Boston.

Via Buffalo or Niagara Falls, Binghamton, Mechanicsville and
Hoosac Tunnel.

* G. 37 Canada Southern R'y to Buffalo or Niagara Falls
N. Y., Lake Erie & West'n R. R. to Binghamton
D. & H. Canal Co.'s R. R. .... to Mechanicsville
Boston, Hoosac Tunnel & West'n R. R. to North
Adams
Fitchburg R. R........ ....to Boston 17.00   18.25

ROUTE 12—To Boston.

Via Buffalo or Niagara Falls, Binghamton, Albany, Springfield
and Worcester.

* G. 798 Canada Southern R'y to Buffalo or Niagara Falls
N. Y., Lake Erie & Western R. R. to Binghamton
Delaware & Hudson Canal Co.'s R. R....to Albany
Boston & Albany R. R.................to Boston   ...   17.00   18.25

* See note on page 64.

ROUTE 13—To Boston.

	From Niagara Falls.	From Detroit.	From Toledo.

Via Buffalo or Niagara Falls, New York, New Haven, Springfield and Worcester.

Form.

* G. 413 Canada Southern R'y to Buffalo or Niagara Falls
N. Y., Lake Erie & Western R. R. to New York
N. Y., N. Haven & Hartford R. R. to Springfield
Boston & Albany R. R.............to Boston 21.00 22.70

POINT L'ILET, TADOUSAC.

ROUTE 14—To Boston.

Via Buffalo or Niagara Falls, New York and any Long Island Steamer Line.

* G. 414 Canada Southern R'y to Buffalo or Niagara Falls
N. Y., Lake Erie & Western R. R. to New York
Any Sound Steamer Line..............to Boston 17.00 18.70

ROUTE 15—To Boston.

Via Buffalo or Niagara Falls, New York and Newport or Fall River.

* G. 646 Canada Southern R'y to Buffalo or Niagara Falls
N. Y., Lake Erie & Western R. R. to New York
Fall River Line St'mer to Newport or Fall River
Old Colony R. R...................to Boston 17.00 18.70

* See note on page 64.

THROUGH RATE

	From Niagara Falls.	From Detroit.	From Toledo.

ROUTE 16—To Boston.

Via Buffalo or Niagara Falls, New York, Stonington and Providence.

Form.
* G. 722 Canada Southern R'y to Buffalo or Niagara Falls
N. Y., Lake Erie & Western R. R. to New York
Stonington Steamboat Co.... ... .to Stonington
New York, Prov. & Boston R. R...to Providence
Boston & Providence R. R.............to Boston 17.00   18.70

ROUTE 17—To Boston.

Via Buffalo or Niagara Falls, New York, New Haven, Springfield and Worcester.

* H. 462 Canada Southern R'y to Buffalo or Niagara Falls
N. Y. Central & Hudson Riv. R. R. to New York
N. Y., N. Haven & Hartford R. R. to Springfield
Boston & Albany R. R.................to Boston   ...   21.00   22.70

ROUTE 18—To Boston.

Via Buffalo or Niagara Falls, New York and Long Island Sound Steamers.

*H. 463 Canada Southern R'y to Buffalo or Niagara Falls
N. Y. Central & Hudson Riv. R. R. to New York
Sound Line Steamer....................to Boston 17.00   18.70

ROUTE 19—To Boston.

Via Buffalo or Niagara Falls, New York and Newport or Fall River.

* H. 645 Canada Southern R'y to Buffalo or Niagara Falls
N. Y. Central & Hudson Riv. R. R. to New York
Fall River Line Steamers to Newport or Fall River
Old Colony R. R.......................to Boston 17.00   18.70

ROUTE 20—To Boston.

Via Buffalo or Niagara Falls, New York, Stonington and Providence.

* H. 721 Canada Southern R'y to Buffalo or Niagara Falls
N. Y. Central & Hudson Riv. R. R. to New York
Stonington Steamboat Co...........to Stonington
N. Y., Providence & Boston R. R. to Providence
Boston & Providence R. R... ....to Boston   17.00   18.70

ROUTE 21—To Cooperstown, N. Y. (Otsego Lake).

Via Buffalo or Niagara Falls and Binghamton.

1009 Ex. Canada Southern R'y to Buffalo or Niagara Falls
N. Y., Lake Erie & West. R'y...to Binghampton
D. & H. Canal Co.'s R. R. to Junc. C. & S. V. R. R.
Cooperst'n & Susquehanna V. R. R. to Cooperst'n 13.20   14.45

* See note on page 64.

ROUTE 22—To Cape May, N. J.

Through Rate

From Niag- From From
ara Falls. Detroit. Toledo.

Via Buffalo or Niagara Falls and Lehigh Valley or Northern Central Routes to Philadelphia.

Form.

Ext. 718 West Jersey R. R. . . . . .to Cape May 18.75 20.00

ROUTE 23—To Cobourg, Canada.

P. 731 Canada So. R'y (*via Niagara Falls*). .to Niagara
Steamer. . . . . .to Toronto
Richelieu & Ont. Nav. Co.'s Steamer to Cobourg 4.25 7.75 9.45

ROUTE 24—To Caldwell, N. Y. (Lake George.)

Via Buffalo or Niagara Falls, Rochester, Schenectady and Saratoga.

1010 Ex. Canada Southern R'y to Buffalo or Niagara Falls
N. Y. Cent.& Hudson River R. R. to Schenectady
Del. & Hudson Canal Co.'s R. R. . .to Glens Falls
Glens Falls Stage. . . . .**to Caldwell** 15.30 16.55

ROUTE 25—To Caldwell, N. Y. (Lake George).

Via Montreal, Plattsburg, Lake Champlain, Fort Ticonderoga.

Via P. 731,1012 Ex.,1013 Ex. **or** 1059 Ex. to Montreal
1011 Ex. Grand Trunk R'y. . . . . .to Rouse's Point *Via Toronto.*
Del. & Hudson Canal Co.'s R. R. . . .to Plattsburg 20.35 23.35 25.05
Champ. Trans. Co.'s Steamer to Ft. Ticonderoga *Via Cape Vincent,*
Delaware & Hudson Canal Co.'s **R. R. to** Baldwin *or Rail to Kingston.*
Lake George Steamer. . . . .**to Caldwell** 21.35 23.05

ROUTE 26—Muskoka Lakes (Can.) to Port Carling and Return.

Via Niagara Falls and Toronto.

1015 Ex. Canada **Southern** R'y. . . . . .to Niagara
Steamer. . . . . .to Toronto
Northern R'y. . . . . .to Gravenhurst
Muskoka Steamers. . . . . .to Port Carling 8.00 17.50 20.50
Return same Route.

ROUTE 27—To Lake Rosseau and Return.

Via Niagara Falls and Toronto.

1015 Ex. Canada Southern R'y. . . . . .to Niagara
Steamer. . . . . .to Toronto
Northern R'y. . . . . .to Gravenhurst
Muskoka Steamers. . . . . .to Rosseau 8.50 18.00 21.00
Return same Route.

ROUTE 28—To Lake Joseph and Return.

THROUGH RATE

	From Niag-ara Falls.	From Detroit.	From Toledo.
Via Niagara Falls and Toronto.			

Form.

1015 Ex. Canada Southern R'y................to Niagara
Steamer............. ....to Toronto
Northern R'y....................to Gravenhurst
Muskoka Steamers................to Lake Joseph   **9.00**   18.50   **21.50**
Return same Route.

ROUTE 29—All Round Lakes.

Via Niagara Falls and Toronto.

1015 Ex. Canada Southern R'y................to Niagara
Steamer............................to Toronto
Northern R'y....................to Gravenhurst
Muskoka Steamer................all round Lakes   9.75   19.25   22.25
Return same Route.

ROUTE 30—To Port Carling and Return.

Via Hagersville and Hamilton.

1014 Ex. Canada Southern R'y.............to Hagersville
Northern & Northwestern R'ys...to Gravenhurst
Muskoka Steamer................to Port Carling   ...   15.60   17.50
Return same Route.

ROUTE 31—To Lake Rosseau and Return.

Via Hagersville and Hamilton.

1014 Ex. Canada Southern R'y.............to Hagersville
Northern & Northwestern R'ys...to Gravenhurst
Muskoka Steamer.....................to Rosseau 16.10   18.00
Return same Route.

ROUTE 32—To Lake Joseph and Return.

Via Hagersville and Hamilton.

1014 Ex. Canada Southern R'y.............to Hagersville
Northern & Northwestern R'ys...to Gravenhurst
Muskoka Steamers................to Lake Joseph **16.60**   18.50
Return same Route.

ROUTE 33—All Round Lakes.

Via Hagersville and Hamilton.

1014 Ex. Canada Southern R'y.............to Hagersville
Northern & Northwestern R'ys...to Gravenhurst
Muskoka Steamer,... ....,...all round Lakes 17.35   19.25
Return same Route,

ROUTE 34—To Montreal.

THROUGH RATE

	From Niagara Falls	From Detroit	From Toledo

Form. **Via Niagara Falls, Toronto, River St. Lawrence Rapids.**

P. 731 Canada Southern R'y .... .to Niagara
Steamer................................to Toronto
Richelieu & Ont. Nav. Co. Steamer..to Montreal   12.00   15.00   16.70

ROUTE 35—To Montreal.

Via Niagara Falls, Toronto, Kingston, and Rail or Steamer.

1012 Ex. Canada Southern R'y ....to Niagara
Steamer ....to Toronto
Grand Trunk R'y........ ....to Kingston
G. T. R'y or Rich. & Ont. N. Co. St'r to Montreal   12.00   15.00   16.70

TADOUSAC, SAGUENAY RIVER.

ROUTE 36—To Montreal.

Via Buffalo or Niagara Falls, Syracuse, Cape Vincent, and Thousand Islands and Rapids.

1013 Ex. Canada Southern R'y to Buffalo or Niagara Falls
N. Y. Central & Hudson River R. R. to Syracuse
Rome, Watertown & Ogd. R. R. to Cape Vincent
Steamer........................to Alexandria Bay
Richelieu & Ont. Nav. Co. Steamer..to Montreal ......_15.00 ^ 16.70

THROUGH RATE
From Niag-   From   From
ara Falls.   Detroit.   Toledo.

ROUTE 37—To Montreal.

Via Niagara Falls, Lewiston, Oswego, Cape Vincent, Thousand Islands
Form.   and Rapids of St. Lawrence.

1059 Ex. Canada Southern R'y...........to Niagara Falls
         N. Y. Central & Hudson River R. R. to Lewiston
         Rome, Watertown & Ogd. R. R. to Cape Vincent
         St. Lawrence Steamboat Co. Steamer to Montreal 15.00   16.70

ROUTE 38—To Montreal.

Via Niagara Falls, Toronto, Prescott and Ottawa.

P. 731   Canada Southern R'y.... ....to Niagara
To Pres- Steamer.............................to Toronto
cott.   Richelieu & Ont. Nav. Co. Steamer ..to Prescott

Ext. 904 St. Lawrence & Ottawa R. R......... ...to Ottawa
         Que., Mon., Otta'a & Occidental R'y to Montreal   12.00   15.00   16.70

ROUTE 39—To New York.

Via Buffalo or Niagara Falls.

* G. 393 Canada Southern R'y to Buffalo or Niagara Falls
         N. Y., Lake Erie & Western R. R. to New York 16.00   17.25

ROUTE 40—To New York.

Via Buffalo or Niagara Falls.

* H. 427 Canada Southern R'y to Buffalo or Niagara Falls
         N. Y. Central & Hudson Riv. R. R. to New York   16.00   17.25

ROUTE 41—To New York.

Via Buffalo or Niagara Falls, Albany and Steamer on Hudson River.

* H. 542 Canada Southern R'y to Buffalo or Niagara Falls
         N. Y. Central & Hudson Riv. R. R....to Albany
         People's Line Steamers.............to New York 14.50   15.75

ROUTE 42—To New York.

Via Buffalo or Niagara Falls, Albany and Steamer on Hudson River.

* H. 543 Canada Southern R'y to Buffalo or Niagara Falls
         N. Y. Central & Hudson Riv. R. R....to Albany
         Day Line Steamers................to New York 15.00   16.25

    * See note on page 64.

ROUTE 43—To New York

THROUGH RATE

From Niag-   From   From
ara Falls.   Detroit.   Toledo.

Via Niagara Falls, Montreal, Plattsburg, Lake Champlain, Saratoga
and Albany.

Form.   Via P. 731,1012 Ex.,1013 Ex. or 1059 Ex. to Montreal
1016 Ex. Grand Trunk R'y...............to Rouse's Point   *Via Toronto.*
     Dela're & Hud'n Canal Co.'s R. R. to Plattsburg   23.00   27.00   28.70
     L. Champ. Trans. Co.'s Steamer to Ft. Ticoderoga   *Via Cape Vincent,*
     Delaware & Hudson Canal Co.'s R. R. to Albany *or Rail to Kingston.*
     N. Y. Central & Hudson Riv. R. R. to New York 24.00   25.70

ROUTE 44—To New York.

Via Niagara Falls, **Montreal,** Plattsburg, **Lake Champlain, Saratoga,**
Albany **and Steamer** on Hudson River.

     Via P. 731,1012 Ex.,1013 Ex. or 1059 Ex. to Montreal
1017 Ex. Grand Trunk R'y...............to Rouse's Point   *Via Toronto.*
     Del. & Hudson Canal **Co.'s** R. R...to Plattsburg   22.20   26.20   27.90
     Lake C. Trans. Co.'s Steamer to Ft. Ticonderoga   *Via Cape Vincent,*
     Delaware & Hudson Canal Co.'s R. R. to Albany *or Rail to Kingston.*
     People's Line Steamer..............to New York 23.20   24.90

ROUTE 45—To New York.

Via Niagara Falls, Montreal, Plattsburg, **Lake** Champlain, Saratoga,
Albany and Steamer on Hudson River.

     Via P. 731,1012 Ex.,1013 Ex. **or** 1059 Ex. to Montreal
1018 Ex. Grand Trunk R'v...............to Rouse's Point   *Via Toronto.*
     Del. & Hudson Canal Co.'s R. R...to Plattsburg   22.70   26.70   28.40
     Lake C. Trans. Co.'s Steamer to Ft. Ticonderoga   *Via Cape Vincent,*
     Delaware & Hudson Canal Co.'s R. R. to Albany *or Rail to Kingston.*
     Day Line Steamer.................to New York 23.70   25.40

ROUTE 46—To New York.

Via Niagara Falls, Montreal, Plattsburg, Lake **Champlain, Lake George,**
Glens Falls, Saratoga, Albany **and Rail.**

     Via P. 731,1012 Ex.,1013 Ex. or 1059 Ex. to Montreal
1019 **Ex.** Grand Trunk R'y...............to Rouse's Point
     Del. & Hudson Canal Co.'s R. R....to Plattsburg
     Lake C. Trans. Co.'s Steamer to Ft. Ticonderoga
     Delaware & Hudson Canal Co.'s R. R. to Baldwin   *Via Toronto.*
     Lake George Steamers.............to Caldwell   26.55   30.55   34.25
     Glens Falls Stage................ to Glens Falls   *Via Cape Vincent,*
     Delaware & Hudson **Canal Co.'s** R. R. to Albany *or Rail to Kingston.*
     N.Y. Central & Hudson **Riv. R. R.** to New York 27.55   29.25

ROUTE 47—To New York.

Via Niagara Falls, Montreal, Plattsburg, Lake Champlain, Lake George, Glens Falls, Saratoga, Albany and Hudson River Steamer.

Form.   Via P. 731, 1012 Ex., 1013 Ex. or 1059 Ex. to Montreal
1020 Ex. Grand Trunk R'y ....to Rouse's Point
Del. & Hudson Canal Co.'s R. R....to Plattsburg
Lake C. Trans. Co.'s Steamer to Ft. Ticonderoga
Delaware & Hudson Canal Co.'s R. R. to Baldwin   *Via Toronto.*
Lake George Steamers..............to Caldwell   25.05   29.05   30.75
Glens Falls Stage..................to Glens Falls *Via Cape Vincent,*
Delaware & Hudson Canal Co.'s R. R. to Albany *or Rail to Kingston.*
People's Line Steamers.............to New York 26.05 27.75

LAKE WINNEPISEOGEE.

ROUTE 48—To New York.

Via Niagara Falls, Montreal, Plattsburg, Lake Champlain, Lake George, Glen's Falls, Saratoga, Albany and Hudson River Steamer.

Via P. 731, 1012 Ex., 1013 Ex. or 1059 Ex. to Montreal
1021 Ex. Grand Trunk R'y ....to Rouse's Point
Delaware & Hud. Canal Co.'s R.R. to Plattsburg
Lake C. Trans. Co.'s Steamer to Ft. Ticonderoga
Delaware & Hudson Canal Co.'s R.R. to Baldwin   *Via Toronto.*
Lake George Steamers ....to Caldwell 25.55 29.55 31.25
Glens Falls Stage................ to Glens Falls *Via Cape Vincent,*
Delaware & Hudson Canal Co.'s R.R. to Albany *or Rail to Kingston.*
Day Line Steamers.................to New York 26.55 28.25

ROUTE 49—To New York.

Via Niagara Falls, Montreal, Newport, White River Junction **and Springfield.**

Form. Via P. 731,1012 Ex.,1013 Ex. or 1059 Ex. to Montreal		
1024 Ex. Southeastern R. R..................to Newport		
Passumpsic R. R...... to White River Junction		
Central Vermont R. R..............to Windsor	*Via Toronto.*	
Vermont Valley R. R..............to Brattleboro	23.00 27.00	28.70
Central Vermont R. R..........to South Vernon	*Via Cape Vincent,*	
Connecticut River R. R...........to Springfield	*or Rail to Kingston.*	
New York, N. H. & Hartford **R. R. to** New York	24.00	25.70

ROUTE 50—To New York.

Via Niagara Falls, Montreal, Quebec, Sherbrooke, White River Junction and Springfield.

Via P. 731,1012 Ex.,1013 Ex. or 1059 Ex. to Montreal		
1025 Ex. Grand Trunk or Richelieu & Ont. N. Co. to Quebec		
Grand Trunk R'y...............to Sherbrooke		
Passumpsic R. R.......**to White River Junction**		
Central Vermont R. R...............to Windsor	*Via Toronto.*	
Vermont Valley R. R.............to Brattleboro	26.00 30.00	31.70
Central Vermont R. R..........to South Vernon	*Via Cape Vincent,*	
Connecticut River R. R...........to Springfield	*or Rail to Kingston.*	
New York, N. H. & Hartford R. R. to New York	27.00	28.70

ROUTE 51—To New York.

	Via Toronto.	
Via Route 1...........................to Boston	25.75 29.75	31.45
1022 Ex. Boston & Albany R. R.............to Springfield	*Via Cape Vincent,*	
	or Rail to Kingston.	
New York, **N. H. &** Hartford R. R. to **New** York	26.75	28.45

ROUTE 52—To New York.

	Via Toronto.	
Via **Route 2**..... ....to Boston	25.75 29.75	31.45
1022 Ex. Boston & Albany R. R.............to Springfield	*Via Cape Vincent,*	
	or Rail to Kingston.	
New York, N. H. & Hartford R. R. to New **York**	26.75	28.45

ROUTE 53—To New York.

	Via Toronto.	
Via Route 3...........................to Boston	25.75 29.75	31.45
1022 Ex. Boston & Albany R. R.............to Springfield	*Via Cape Vincent,*	
	or Rail to Kingston.	
New York, N. H. & Hartford R. R. to New York	26.75	28.45

THROUGH RATE

ROUTE 54—To New York.

	From Niagara Falls.	From Detroit.	From Toledo.

Via Toronto.

Form. Via Route 4.............................to Boston 29.75 33.75 35.45
1022 Ex. Boston & Albany R. R.............to Springfield *Via Cape Vincent,*
New York, N. H. & Hartford R. R. to New York ...... *or Rail to Kingston.* 30.75 **32.45**

ROUTE 55—To New York.

Via Toronto.

Via Route 5....................... ....to Boston 28.75 32.75 34.45
1022 Ex. Boston & Albany R. R.............to Springfield *Via Cape Vincent,*
New York, N. H. & Hartford R. R. to New York ...... *or Rail to Kingston.* 29.75 31.45

ROUTE 56—To New York.

Via Toronto.

Via Route 6.............................to Boston 34.40 37.40 39.10
1022 Ex. Boston & Albany R. R.............to Springfield *Via Cape Vincent,*
New York, N. H. & Hartford R. R. to New York ... .. *or Rail to Kingston.* 35.40 37.10

ROUTE 57—To New York.

Via Toronto.

Via Route 7.............................to Boston 34.25 37.25 39.00
1022 Ex. Boston & Albany R. R........ ....to Springfield *Via Cape Vincent,*
New York, N. H. & Hartford R. R. to New York *or Rail to Kingston.* 35.25 37.00

ROUTE 58—To New York.

Via Route 8.............................to Boston
*1022 Ex. Boston & Albany R. R............to Springfield
New York, N. H. & Hartford R. R. to New York 22.75 24.00

ROUTE 59—To New York.

Via Route 9.............................to Boston
*1022 Ex. Boston & Albany R. R............to Springfield
New York, N. H. & Hartford R. R. to New York . . 22.75 24.00

ROUTE 60—To New York.

Via Route 10.............................to Boston
*1022 Ex. Boston & Albany R. R............to Springfield
New York, N. H. & Hartford R. R. to New York ... 22.75 24.00

* See note on page 64.

	THROUGH RATE		
	From Niagara Falls.	From Detroit.	From Toledo.

ROUTE 61—To New York.

Form. Via Route 11.........................to Boston
*1022 Ex. Boston & Albany R. R............to Springfield
New York, N. H. & Hartford R. R. to New York 22.75 24.00

ROUTE 62—To New York.

Via Route 12..........................to Boston
*1022 Ex. Boston & Albany R. R............to Springfield
New York, N. H. & Hartford R. R. to New York 22.75 24.00

ROUTE 63—To New York.

Via Toronto.
Via Route 1..........................to Boston 24.00 28.00 29.70
1023 Ex. Old Colony R. R......to Fall River or Newport *Via Cape Vincent,*
or Rail to Kingston.
Fall River Line Steamer............to New York 25.00 26.70

ROUTE 64—To New York.

Via Toronto.
Via Route 2..........................to Boston 24.00 28.00 29.70
1023 Ex. Old Colony R. R......to Fall River or Newport *Via Cape Vincent,*
or Rail to Kingston.
Fall River Line Steamer............to New York 25.00 26.70

ROUTE 65—To New York.

Via Toronto.
Via Route 3..........................to Boston 24.00 28.00 29.70
1023 Ex. Old Colony R. R......to Fall River or Newport *Via Cape Vincent,*
or Rail to Kingston.
Fall River Line Steamer............to New York 25.00 26.70

ROUTE 66—To New York.

Via Toronto.
Via Route 4..........................to Boston 28.00 32.00 33.70
1023 Ex. Old Colony R. R......to Fall River or Newport *Via Cape Vincent,*
or Rail to Kingston.
Fall River Line Steamer...........to New York 29.00 30.70

ROUTE 67—To New York.

Via Toronto.
Via Route 5..........................to Boston 27.00 31.00 32.70
1023 Ex. Old Colony R. R.......to Fall River or Newport *Via Cape Vincent,*
or Rail to Kingston.
Fall River Line Steamer..........to New York 28.00 29.70

* See note on page 64.

MAPLEWOOD HOTEL, BETHLEHEM, N. H

THROUGH RATE

	From Niag- ara Falls.	From Detroit.	From Toledo.

ROUTE 68—To New York.

Via Toronto.

Form. Via Route 6...........................to Boston 32.65 35.65 37.35

1023 Ex. Old Colony R. R.......to Fall River or Newport *Via Cape Vincent,*
or Rail to Kingston.

Fall River Line Steamer.   ..to New York 33.65 35.35

ROUTE 69—To New York.

Via Toronto.

Via Route 7.............   .to Boston 32.50 35.50 37.25

1023 Ex. Old Colony R. R.......to Fall River or Newport *Via Cape Vincent,*
or Rail to Kingston.

Fall River Line Steamer..   ..to New York 33.50 35.25

ROUTE 70—To New York.

Via Route 8........... ....to Boston

*1023 Ex. Old Colony R. R......to Fall River or Newport

Fall River Line Steamer...........to New York 21.00 22.25

ROUTE 71—To New York.

Via Route 9...........................to Boston

*1023 Ex. Old Colony R. R.....to Fall River or Newport

Fall River Line Steamer...........to New York 21.00 **22.25**

ROUTE 72—To New York.

Via Route 10...........................to Boston

*1023 Ex. Old Colony R. R......to Fall River or Newport

Fall River Line Steamer....... ... ...to New York 21.00 22.25

ROUTE 73—To New York.

Via Route 11...........................to Boston

*1023 Ex. Old Colony R. R.....to Fall River or Newport

Fall River Line Steamer.... ....to New York 21.00 22.25

ROUTE 74—To New York.

Via Route 12.. ....to Boston

*1023 Ex. Old Colony R. R......to Fall River or Newport

Fall River Line Steamer.... ....to New York 21.00 22.25

* See note on page 64.

THROUGH **RATE**

From Niag-   From   From
ara Falls.   Detroit. Toledo.
Via Toronto.

ROUTE 75—To New York.

Form. Via Route 1..........................to Boston   24.00   28.00   29.70
*1004 Ex. Boston & Providence R. R........to Providence   *Via Cape Vincent,*
N. Y., Providence & Boston R. R. to Stonington   *or Rail to Kingston.*
Stonington Steamboat Co.   to New York 25.00   26.70

ROUTE 76—To New York.

Via Toronto.

Via Route 2........... ....to Boston   24.00   28.00   29.70
1004 **Ex.** Boston & Providence R. R........to Providence   *Via Cape Vincent,*
New York, Prov. & Boston **R. R**...**to** Stonington   *or Rail to Kingston.*
Stonington Steamboat Co...........**to** New York 25.00   26.70

ROUTE 77—To New York.

Via Toronto.

Via Route 3. ....to Boston   24.00   28.00   29.00
1004 Ex. Boston & Providence R. R....... .to Providence   *Via Cape Vincent,*
New York, Prov. & Boston **R**. R...to Stonington   *or Rail to Kingston.*
Stonington Steamboat Co...........to New York 25.00   26.70

ROUTE 78—To New York.

Via Toronto.

Via Route 4...........................to Boston   28.00   32.00   33.70
1004 **Ex.** Boston **&** Providence R. R........to Providence   *Via Cape Vincent,*
New York, Prov. & Boston **R. R**...to Stonington   *or Rail to Kingston.*
Stonington Steamboat Co...........to New York 29.00   30.70

ROUTE 79—To New York.

Via Toronto.

Via Route 5...........................to Boston   27.00   31.00   32.70
1004 **Ex.** Boston & Providence R. R........to Providence   *Via Cape Vincent,*
New York, Prov. & Boston **R. R**...to Stonington   *or Rail to Kingston.*
Stonington Steamboat Co...........to New York 28.00   29.70

ROUTE 80—To New York.

Via Toronto.

Via Route 6...........................to Boston   32.65   35.65   37.35
1004 **Ex. Boston & Providence R. R**........to Providence   *Via Cape Vincent,*
New York, Prov. & Boston R. R...to Stonington   *or Rail to Kingston.*
Stonington Steamboat Co...........to New York   ...   33.65   35.35

* See note on page 64.

ROUTE 81—To New York.

		THROUGH RATE		
		From Niagara Falls.	From Detroit.	From Toledo.
		Via Toronto.		
Form.	Via Route 7..................................to Boston	32.50	35.50	37.25
1004	Ex. Boston & Providence R. R...........to Providence	*Via Cape Vincent,*		
	New York, Prov. & Boston R. R...to Stonington	*or Rail to Kingston.*		
	Stonington Steamboat Co............to New York	......	33.50	35.25

ROUTE 82—To New York.

Via Route 8......................to Boston	
*1004 Ex. Boston & Providence R. R........to Providence	
New York, Prov. & Boston R. R...to Stonington	
Stonington Steamboat Co... ....to New York	21.00 22.25

ROUTE 83—To New York.

Via Route 9........................... to Boston	
*1004 Ex. Boston & Providence R. R........to Providence	
New York, Prov. & Boston R. R...to Stonington	
Stonington Steamboat Co...........to New York	21.00 22.25

ROUTE 84—To New York.

Via Route 10..........................to Boston	
*1004 Ex. Boston & Providence R. R........to Providence	
New York, Prov. & Boston R. R. to Stonington	
Stonington Steamboat Co...........to New York	21.00 22.25

ROUTE 85—To New York.

Via Route 11..........................to Boston	
*1004 Ex. Boston & Providence R. R.......to Providence	
New York, Prov. & Boston R. R...to Stonington	
Stonington Steamboat Co...........to New York	21.00 22.25

ROUTE 86—To New York.

Via Route 12..........................to Boston	
*1004 Ex. Boston & Providence R. R........to Providence	
New York, Prov. & Boston R. R...to Stonington	
Stonington Steamboat Co...........to New York	21.00 22.25

ROUTE 87—To Newport, R. I.

Via Buffalo or Niagara Falls, Albany, Worcester and Providence.

H. 743 Canada So. R'y.......to Buffalo or Niagara Falls	
New York Cen. & H. River R. R......to Albany	
Boston & Albany R. R..............to Worcester	
Providence & Worcester R. R.....to Providence	
Newport Steamer....................to Newport	17.25 18.50

* See note on page 64.

PROFILE HOUSE, FRANCONIA MOUNTAINS.

ROUTE 88—To Portland, Me.

THROUGH RATE

	From Niagara Falls.	From Detroit.	From Toledo.

Via Toronto.

Form. Via P.731, 1012 Ex., 1013 Ex. or 1059 Ex. to Montreal 18.50 22.50 24.20

Via Cape Vincent, or Rail to Kingston.

1005 Ex. Grand Trunk R'y... to Portland 19.50 21.20

ROUTE 88½—To Portland, Me.

Via Montreal, St. Johnsbury and Fabyans.

Via P.731, 1012 Ex., 1013 Ex. or 1059 Ex. to Montreal
1027 Ex. Southeastern R'y.....................to Newport
Passumpsic R. R.....................to St. Johnsbury *Via Toronto.*
St. Johnsb'y & Lake Champ. R. R. to Lunenburg 18.50 22.50 24.20
Portland & Ogdensburg R. R.....to Scott's Mills *Via Cape Vincent,*
Boston, Concord & Montreal R. R....to Fabyans *or Rail to Kingston.*
Portland & Ogdensburg R. R.........to Portland 19.50 21.20

ROUTE 89—To Portland, Me.

Via Montreal, Quebec, Sherbrooke and Gorham.

Via Toronto.
Via P.731, 1012 Ex., 1013 Ex. or 1059 Ex. to Montreal 21.50 25.50 27.20
1029 Ex. G. T. R'y or Rich. & Ont. Nav. Co.....to Quebec *Via Cape Vincent,*
or Rail to Kingston.
Grand Trunk R'y.....................to Portland 22.50 24.20

ROUTE 90—To Portland, Me.

Via Montreal, Quebec, St. Johnsbury and Fabyans.

Via P. 731, 1012 Ex., 1013 Ex. or 1059 Ex. to Montreal
1028 Ex. G. T. R'y or Rich. & Ont. Nav. Co.....to Quebec
Grand Trunk R'y...............to Sherbrooke
Passumpsic R. R.................to St. Johnsbury *Via Toronto.*
St. Johnsb'y & Lake Champ. R. R. to Lunenburg 21.50 25.50 27.20
Portland & Ogdensburg R. R.....to Scott's Mills *Via Cape Vincent,*
Boston, Concord & Montreal R.R....to Fabyans *or Rail to Kingston.*
Portland & Ogdensburg R. R........to Portland 22.50 24.20

ROUTE 91—To Portland, Me.

Via Buffalo or Niagara Falls, Troy, Hoosac Tunnel and Boston.

H. 538 Canada Southern R'y to Buffalo or Niagara Falls
New York Central & Hudson River R. R. to Troy
Troy & Boston R. R.............to North Adams
Fitchburg R. R.... ....to Boston
Boston & Maine R. R..............to Portland 20.25 21.50

ROUTE 92—To Portland, Me.

		THROUGH RATE		
		From Niagara Falls.	From Detroit.	From Toledo.
Form.	Same as Route 91 to Boston.			
H. 666	Eastern R. R.........................to Portland	20.25	21.50	

ROUTE 93—To Portland, Me.

Via Buffalo or Niagara Falls, Albany and Boston.

H. 562	Canada Southern R'y to Buffalo or Niagara Falls			
	N. Y. Central & Hudson River R. R...to Albany			
	Boston & Albany R. R.................to Boston			
	Boston & Maine R. R.................to Portland	20.25	21.50	

ROUTE 94—To Portland, Me.

Same as Route 93 to Boston.

H. 503	Eastern R. R................. ....to Portland	20.25	21.50	

ROUTE 95—To Portland, Me.

Via Buffalo or Niagara Falls, Troy, Hoosac Tunnel, Ayer Junction and Rochester, N. H.

H. 770	Canada Southern R'y to Buffalo or Niagara Falls			
	New York Central & Hudson River R. R. to Troy			
	Troy & Boston R. R.............to North Adams			
	Fitchburg R. R.... ....to Ayer Junction			
	Worcester & Nashua R. R..........to Rochester			
	Portland & Rochester R. R...... ....to Portland	20.25	21.50	

ROUTE 96—To Quebec, P. Q.

Via Niagara Falls, St. Lawrence River and Montreal.

	Via P. 731,1012 Ex.,1013 Ex. or 1059 Ex. to Montreal			
1030 Ex.	G. T. R'y or Richelieu & Ont. Nav. Co. to Quebec	14.00	17.00	18.70

ROUTE 97—To Saratoga, N. Y.

Via Niagara Falls, Montreal, Plattsburg and Lake Champlain.

	Via P. 731,1012 Ex.,1013 Ex. or 1059 Ex. to Montreal	*Via Toronto.*		
1035 Ex.	Grand Trunk R'y................to Rouse's Point	19.75	23.75	25.45
	Delaware & Hud. Canal Co.'s R. R. to Plattsburg	*Via Cape Vincent,*		
	Lake Champlain Steamers....to Ft. Ticonderoga	*or Rail to Kingston.*		
	Delaware & Hudson Canal Co.'s R. R. to Saratoga	20.75	22.45	

ROUTE 98—To Saratoga, N. Y.

THROUGH RATE

From Niag- From From
ara Falls. Detroit. Toledo.

Via Niagara Falls, Montreal, **Lake** Champlain and Lake George.

Form.	Via P. 731,1012 Ex.,1013 Ex. or 1059 Ex. to Montreal			
1036 Ex.	Grand Trunk R'y.............to Rouse's Point			
	Delaware & Hud. Canal Co.'s R. R. to Plattsburg			
	Lake Champlain Steamers....to Ft. Ticonderoga	*Via Toronto.*		
	Delaware & Hudson Canal Co.'s R. R. to Baldwin	22.35	26.65	28.10
	Lake George Steamers.............to Caldwell	*Via Cape Vincent,*		
	Glens Falls Stage...,...........to Glens Falls	*or Rail to Kingston.*		
	Delaware & Hudson Canal Co.'s R. R. to Saratoga	23.35	25.10	

ROUTE 99—To Saratoga, N. Y.

Via Buffalo or Niagara Falls, Rochester and Schenectady.

H. 54	Canada Southern R'y to Buffalo or Niagara Falls		
	N. Y. Central & Hud. Riv. R. R. to Schenectady		
	Delaware & Hudson Canal Co.'s R. R. to Saratoga	16.40	17.05

ROUTE 100—To St. Catherines, Ont.

J. 467	Canada Southern R'y.................to Welland		
	Welland R'y...................to St. Catherines	6.65	7.90

ROUTE 101—To Toronto, Ont.

Via Niagara Falls.

P. 544	Canada Southern R'y.................to Niagara			
	Steamer................................to Toronto	2.00	7.00	8.70

ROUTE 102—To Thousand Islands (Alexandria Bay.)

Via Niagara Falls, **Toronto** and **Kingston**.

1038 Ex.	Canada Southern R'y.................to Niagara			
	Steamer................................to Toronto			
	Richelieu & Ont. Nav. Co. Steamer..to Kingston			
	Richelieu & Ont. N. Co. Stmr.to Alexandria Bay	8.50	12.00	13.70

ROUTE 103—To Thousand Islands (Alexandria Bay.)

Via Buffalo **or** Niagara **Falls, Syracuse and** Cape Vincent.

1039 Ex.	Canada Southern R'y to Buffalo or Niagara Falls		
	New York Cen. & H. River R. R.. .to Syracuse		
	Rome, W. & Ogdensburg R. R..to Cape Vincent		
	Steamer.....................to Alexandria Bay	12.00	13.70

ROUTE 104—To Thousand Islands (Alexandria Bay.)

THROUGH RATE

	From Niagara Falls.	From Detroit.	From Toledo.

Form. Via Niagara Falls, Lewiston, Oswego and Cape Vincent.

1060 Ex. Canada Southern R'y...........to Niagara Falls
New York Cen. & H. River R. R....to Lewiston
Rome, W. & Ogdensburg R. R...to Cape Vincent
St. L. Steamboat Co's Stmr....to Alexandria Bay 12.00 13.70

ROUTE 105—To Watkins Glen, N. Y.

Via Buffalo or Niagara Falls and Canandaigua.

II. 104   Canada So. R'y.......to Buffalo or Niagara Falls
New York Cen. & H. Riv. R. R. to Canandaigua
Northern Central R. R...............to Watkins   9.90   11.15

ROUTE 106—To Wyandotte, Mich.

White Sulphur Springs.

Local.   Canada Southern R'y...to Wyandotte and Return   11.90   .50   2.50

SIDE TRIPS.

ROUTE 107.

New York to Boston, vía Fall River Line.

Form.	*To be issued in connection with ticket to New York.*	RATE.
1047 Ex.	Fall River Line Steamers.......... ....to Newport or Fall River	
	Old Colony R.R............. ....to Boston	4.00

ROUTE 108.

New York to Boston, via Stonington Line.

To be issued in connection with ticket to New York.

1048 Ex.	Stonington Line Steamers....................to Stonington	
	New York, Providence & Boston R. R..........to Providence	
	Boston & Providence R. R....................to Boston	4.00

ROUTE 109.

New York to Boston, via Shore Line, all rail.

To be issued in connection with ticket to New York.

1049 Ex.	New York, New Haven & Hartford R. R.......to New Haven	
	N. York, N. Haven & Hart. R. R. (Hartford Div.), to Springfield	
	Boston & Albany R. R....................to Boston	5.75

ROUTE 110.

Weirs to Centre Harbor and Return, (Lake Winnepiseogee).

1058 Ex.	Steamer "Lady of the Lake,"....to Centre Harbor and Return	.50

ROUTE 111.

Newport to Magog and Return, (Lake Memphremagog).

1055 Ex.	Steamer "Lady of the Lake,"............to Magog and Return	1.00

ROUTE 112.

St. Johnsbury to Fabyans.

1057 Ex.	St. Johnsbury and Lake Champlain.............to Lunenburg	
	Portland & Ogdensburg R. R...................to Scott's Mills	
	Boston, Concord & Montreal R. R................. to Fabyans	1.85

CITY OF QUEBEC.

ROUTE 113.

Form. **St. Johnsbury to Fabyans and Return to Wells River.** RATE.

1056 Ex. St. Johnsbury & Lake Champlain R. R..........to Lunenburg
Portland & Ogdensburg R. R...................to Scott's Mills
Boston, Concord & Montreal R. R.............. ...to Fabyans
Boston, Concord & Montreal R. R,.. ....to Wells River   3.85

ROUTE 114.

Fabyans to Summit of Mount Washington and Return.

1053 Ex. Boston, Concord & Montreal R. R. to Base of Mt. Washington
Mount Washington R. R...........Base to Summit and Return
Boston, Concord & Montreal R. R.................to Fabyans   6.00

ROUTE 115.

Fabyans to Summit of Mount Washington and Return to Wells River.

1054 Ex. Boston, Concord & Montreal R. R. to Base of Mt. Washington
Mount Washington R. R................to Summit and Return
Boston, Concord & Montreal R. R.............to Wells River   8.00

ROUTE 116.

Providence to Narragansett Pier, R. I., and Return.

1050 Ex. New York, Providence & Boston R. R.............to Kingston
Narragansett Pier R. R...................to Narragansett Pier
Narragansett Pier R. R.........................to Kingston
New York, Providence & Boston R. R..........to Providence   1.75

ROUTE 117.

New York to Newport.

1063 Ex. Old Colony Steamboat Company (Fall River Line) to Newport   3.00

ROUTE 118.

Boston to Old Orchard Beach and Return.

1051 Ex. Boston & Maine R. R.. ....to Old Orchard Beach
Boston & Maine R. R.............................to Boston   4.00

ROUTE 119.

Portland to Old Orchard Beach and Return.

1026 Ex. Boston & Maine R. R...................to Old Orchard Beach
Boston & Maine R. R...........................to Portland   .60

ROUTE 120.

Form.   Bethlehem **to Profile House and** Return.   RATE.

1052 Ex. Profile & Franconia Notch **R. R**...............to Profile House
Profile & Franconia Notch **R. R**.............. ...to Bethlehem   3.00

ROUTE 121.

Montreal **to** Quebec and Return.

1031 **Ex.** G. T. R'y or Richelieu & Ont. Nav. Co.'s Steamer...to Quebec
G. T. R'y or Richelieu & Ont. Nav. Co.'s Steamer..to Montreal   4.00

ROUTE 122.

Montreal **to** Quebec and Return.

Ext. 903 Quebec, Montreal, Ottawa & Occidental R'y........to Quebec
Quebec, Montreal, Ottawa & Occidental R'y ......to Montreal   4.00

ROUTE 123.

Utica to Richfield Springs and Return.

1032 Ex. Delaware, **Lakawana & Western R. R**.....to Richfield Springs
Delaware, **Lakawana & Western R. R**...............to Utica   1.50

ROUTE 124.

Boston to Rye Beach and Return.

1033 Ex. Eastern **R. R**...................................to North Hampton
Stage................. ....to Rye Beach
Stage....................................**to** North Hampton
Eastern **R. R**..to Boston   3.50

ROUTE 125.

Portland to Rye Beach and Return.

1034 **Ex.** Eastern R. R................................to North Hampton
Stage................................. ....to Rye Beach
Stage.................................to North Hampton
Eastern R. R..to Portland   4.50

ROUTE 126.

Albany to Sharon Springs and Return.

1037 Ex. Delaware & Hudson **Canal Co's R. R**...... to Sharon Springs
Delaware & Hudson **Canal Co's R. R**...............to Albany   2.50

ROUTE 127.

Form.	**Binghampton to Sharon Springs and Return.**	RATE.
10½ Ex.	Delaware & Hudson Canal Co's R. R........to Sharon Springs	
	Delaware & Hudson Canal Co's R. R..........to Binghampton	6.35

ROUTE 128.

Lower St. Lawrence River—Quebec to **Riviere Du Loup and Return,**
(Cacouna.)

1061 Ex.	**St.** Lawrence Steam Navigaton Co's. Stmr to Riviere Du Loup	
	St. Lawrence Steam Navigation Co's Steamer........to Quebec	4.00

ROUTE 129.

Quebec to Murray Bay and Return.

1062 Ex.	St. Lawrence Steam Navigation **Co's Steamer**...to Murray Bay	
	St. Lawrence Steam Navigation **Co's Steamer**........to Quebec	4.00

ROUTE 130.

Saguenay River—Quebec to Tadousac and Return.

1062 Ex.	**St.** Lawrence Steam Navigation Co's **Steamer**......to Tadousac	
	St. Lawrence Steam Navigation **Co's Steamer**........to Quebec	5.00

ROUTE 131.

Quebec to Ha Ha Bay and Return.

1062 Ex.	**St. Lawrence Steam** Navigation **Co's** Steamer....to Ha Ha Bay	
	St. **Lawrence Steam** Navigation Co's Steamer........to Quebec	8.00

RETURN FORMS.

ROUTE 132—From Montreal.

Form.		THROUGH RATE		
		To Niagara Falls.	To Detroit.	To Toledo.
1043 Ex. Grand Trunk R'y......................to Detroit			15.00	16.70

ROUTE 133—From Montreal.

	To Niagara Falls.	To Detroit.	To Toledo.
1042 Ex. Grand Trunk R'y..................... to Toronto			
Steamer............................ ...to Niagara			
Canada Southern R'y ....to.............	12.00	15.00	16.70

ROUTE 134—From Boston.

	To Niagara Falls.	To Detroit.	To Toledo.
*1041 Ex. Eastern R. R.. ... .to North Conway			
Portland & Ogdensburg R. R........to Fabyans			
Boston, Concord & Montreal R. R. to Scott's Mills			
Portland & Ogdensburg R. R......to Lunenburg			
St. Johnsbury & L. Champ. R. R. to St. Johnsbury			
Passumpsic R. R....................to Newport			
Southeastern R. R.... ....to Montreal			
Via Form 1042 Ex. ....to.............			
Or " 1043 " ....to Detroit		15.00	16.70

ROUTE 135—From Boston.

	To Niagara Falls.	To Detroit.	To Toledo.
*1040 Ex. Boston & Lowell R. R............ ...to Nashua			
Concord R. R......................to Concord			
Boston, Concord & Montreal R. R. to Wells Riv.			
Passumpsic R. R....................to Newport			
Southeastern R. R.....-..........to Montreal			
Via Form 1042 Ex.............to.............			
Or " 1043 " ....to Detroit		15.00	16.70

ROUTE 136—From Boston.

	To Niagara Falls.	To Detroit.	To Toledo.
*H.449 R. Boston & Albany R. R...............to Albany			
N.Y. C. & H. Riv. R.R. to Buffalo or Susp. Bridge			
Canada Southern R'y ....to..........	17.00	18.25	

* See note on page 64.

Form.	ROUTE 137—From Boston.	THROUGH RATE		
		To Niagara Falls.	To Detroit.	To Toledo.
*H.659 R.	Fitchburg R. R.................to North Adams Troy & Boston R. R.....................to Troy N.Y.C. & H. Riv. R.R. to Buffalo or Susp. Bridge Canada Southern R'y ....to............		17.00	18.25

ROUTE 138—From Boston.

*H.645 R.	Old Colony R. R......to Fall River or Newport Fall River Line Steamers..........to New York N.Y.C. & H. Riv. R. R. to Buffalo or Niag. Falls Canada Southern R'y ....to.........		17.00	18.70

ROUTE 139.—From Portland.

*1044 Ex.	Boston & Maine or Eastern R. R..... to Boston Boston & Albany R. R,. ....to Albany N. Y. C. & H. R. R. R. to Buffalo or Susp Bridge Canada Southern R'y............to..		20.00	21.50

ROUTE 140.—From Portland.

*1045 Ex.	Boston & Maine or Eastern R. R......to Boston Fitchburg R. R.................to North Adams Troy & Boston R. R....................to Troy N. Y. C. & H. R. R. R. to Buffalo or Susp. Bridge Canada Southern R'y. ....to.............		20.00	21.50

ROUTE 141.—From Portland.

*1046 Ex.	Portland & Ogdensburg R. R........to Fabyans Boston, Concord & Montreal R. R. to Scott's Mills Portland & Ogdensburg R. R......to Lunenburg St. Johnsbury & L. Champ. R. R. to St. Johnsbury Passumpsic R. R....................to Newport South-Eastern R. R.................to Montreal Via Form 1042 Ex................to............... Or Form 1043 Ex.................to Detroit		22.50	24.20

ROUTE 142—From Philadelphia.

*G. 401 R.	Philadelphia & Reading R. R......to Bethlehem Lehigh Valley R. R..................to Waverly N.Y.,L. E. & W. R. R. to Buffalo or Susp. Bridge Canada Southern R'y....... ....to.............		16.00	17.52

* See note on page 64.

ROUTE 143—From Philadelphia.

Form.

	To Niagara Falls.	To Detroit.	To Toledo.
THROUGH RATE			

*II. 441 R. Pennsylvania R. R..............to Harrisburg
Northern Central R. R............ ....to Sunbury
Pennsylvania R. R. (P. & E. Div.) to Williamsport
Northern Central R. R...........to Canandaigua
N. Y. C. & H. R. R. R...to Buffalo or Susp. Bridge
Canada Southern R'y........ ....to........... .... 16,00 17.25

ROUTE 144—From New York.

*H. 427 R. N. Y. C. & H. R. R. R. to Buffalo or Niagara F.
Canada Southern R'y..... ....to........... ...... 16.00 17.25

ROUTE 145—From New York.

*G. 393 R. N. Y., L. E. & W. R'y to Buffalo or Niagara F.
Canada Southern R'y..............to........... ...... 16.00 17.25

ROUTE 146—From New York.

*S. 428 R. Day Line Steamers....................to Albany
N. Y. C. & H. R. R. R..to Buffalo or Niagara F.
Canada Southern R'y.... ....to.............. ...... 15.00 16.50

---

* Forms marked thus are to be sold only as parts of round-trip tickets, and must read via Montreal one way, either going or coming. They must not be sold as single-trip tickets at rates given in this book. See regular tariff for single-trip rates.

www.ingramcontent.com/pod-product-compliance
Lightning Source LLC
Chambersburg PA
CBHW021530090426
42739CB00007B/868